T H E

PRAYER

O F

JESUS

JOURNAL

THE
PRAYER
OF
JESUS

JOURNAL

An Everyday Adventure
with the Father

KEN HEMPHILL

BROADMAN
&HOLMAN
PUBLISHERS

Nashville, Tennesse

THE PRAYER OF JESUS JOURNAL

0-8054-2666-3

Published by Broadman & Holman Publishers,
Nashville, Tennessee

PREFACE

When the disciples asked Jesus how to pray, He responded with a simple prayer that has never been forgotten. We know it today as the Lord's Prayer.

- The focus of this prayer is on the Father.
- The promises of the prayer represent total provision.

But what is usually less understood by those who have grown up with this prayer as an empty habit or church ritual is that the Lord's Prayer provides a framework for daily living and personal worship. It is an ongoing experience with God. By keeping its truths before us moment by moment, every day becomes an adventure with the Father.

That's what this journal is designed to help you do: to track the transforming power of the Lord's Prayer in your daily life.

Each day for seven weeks, you'll focus on a specific, familiar phrase from the Lord's Prayer. There will be a brief Scripture to read and a few ideas to think about. Then you'll have a chance to be watching for God to make this truth come alive—that very day—through an encounter with someone, an offhand comment, an unexpected twist, a moment God uses to deepen your relationship with Him and to place you in the center of His will.

This is not a workbook where you get points for having the right answers. This journal is a living snapshot of your life—a picture of who the Father really is, what your life can really be like in Him, and how this all plays out in the real-life drama of each and every day.

I've also included a circulating list of seven "Kingdom Accountability Questions" which flow out of the Lord's Prayer—one for each day. Some of the answers to these questions may be very personal. That's why I haven't given you a lot of space in this journal to write out your responses to these questions. But it is important to keep them in the back of your mind as you journey together with God. If you are blessed to have a Christian friend or small group with whom you can meet regularly and share honestly from your heart, these seven questions can form an accountability bond between you and help each of you keep your lives focused on the Father's business. I'll talk with you in more detail about these later.

As you travel through this 7-week adventure with the Father, you'll find yourself recalling select phrases from the prayer of Jesus throughout the day, whispering them back to God, and noticing His near presence in even the most ordinary times and circumstances. You'll find yourself thinking less about yourself and more about others. You'll find yourself seeking His kingdom, yet finding your own needs met in fuller, richer ways than ever before.

I can't wait to hear what God does in your life as you discover—through the gift of the Lord's Prayer—how much the Father loves you and those around you. I know how radically He's changed my life through the prayer of Jesus. I'm sure He will do the same in yours.

Ken Hemphill

THE PRAYER OF JESUS

Our Father which art in heaven,
Hallowed be thy name.
Thy kingdom come.
Thy will be done
in earth, as it is in heaven.
Give us this day our daily bread.
And forgive us our debts,
as we forgive our debtors.
And lead us not into temptation,
but deliver us from evil:
For thine is the kingdom,
and the power, and the glory,
for ever. Amen.

Matthew 6:9–13 (KJV)

CHILDREN OF PRIVILEGE

SCRIPTURE

Because you are sons, God has sent the Spirit of His Son into our hearts, crying, "*Abba, Father!*" So you are no longer a slave, but a son; and if a son, then an heir through God.

Galatians 4:6-7

Stop and consider what an incredible privilege it is to be a child of God, an heir of His boundless riches in glory.

To be an heir in God's family means that His heavenly resources are available to us this very day, enabling us to experience victory in our Christian living.

We are not slaves to Him. We are His children—children who can climb into our Father's lap and receive His love, approval, and blessing.

How can I invest the riches of my Father's inheritance?

Showing His Great Love in my life so that others can grow and his Glory will shine in me that I might lead someone to the Father.

I will be able to live such that when my time on Earth is finished and I stand in front of the Cross I will be able to say I did my Best, I love God + this to my Children + Grandchildren will be my legacy forever in the arms of Christ.

Sept 18, 2012
Sandons
B-Day

This is what God showed me about our relationship today:

That I am so unworthy of my salvation but that he freely gives it to me. That he Gave his Only Son that I might have this salvation! I am so truly Blessed my words are so feeble when trying to Thank God for his Son, Jesus.

Thank-you oh preecious Holy one that I might show myself Worthy to be your child.

Abba, Father, Jesus Son of God I praise your Holy names and seek you, + your Will for my life I ask forgiveness of all the Sins of this day as well as this night. Probetus.

KINGDOM ACCOUNTABILITY QUESTION:

How is my life bringing honor to the Father's name?

I have to think and study this one for now at this moment I am not sure that it has brought Honor to my Father's Name?

WHAT THEY SEE IN ME

SCRIPTURE

"When they came to the nations where they went, they profaned My holy name, for it was said about them, 'These are the LORD's people, yet they had to go out of His land.' "
Ezekiel 36:20

The prophet Ezekiel writes of a time when Israel's behavior was such that they had profaned the Lord's name. Because of their disobedience, God had allowed them to be taken into captivity.

People in the surrounding nations had concluded that Israel's God was not very powerful because He could not protect His own people. They *should* have seen Israel relying on God, living by faith in His delivering power.

What should others conclude about God based on my life?

_____

_____

_____

_____

_____

_____

_____

_____

_____

I saw today how my behavior reflects on the Father's name:

_____

_____

_____

_____

_____

_____

_____

_____

_____

_____

_____

_____

_____

_____

Kingdom Accountability Question:

How am I bringing reproach on my Father's name?

_____

_____

_____

_____

_____

WEEK ONE, DAY THREE

TELL US WHAT YOU KNOW

SCRIPTURE

What we have seen and heard we also declare to you, so that you may have fellowship along with us; and indeed our fellowship is with the Father and with His Son Jesus Christ.

1 John 1:3

God's kingdom is expanded every time the love of Christ is experienced in the heart of another individual.

When was the last time you told someone about your personal relationship with Christ? When we proclaim His salvation, we extend to others a life of unfailing fellowship with the Father and His Son. One of the best ways to participate in God's kingdom activity is through our personal witness.

What keeps me from being more free with my testimony?

_____

_____

_____

_____

_____

_____

_____

_____

I told someone today about what Jesus has done for me:

_____

_____

_____

_____

_____

_____

_____

_____

_____

_____

_____

_____

_____

_____

KINGDOM ACCOUNTABILITY QUESTION:

How well am I responding to kingdom opportunities?

_____

_____

_____

_____

_____

WEEK ONE, DAY FOUR

ACTIONS
SPEAK LOUDER

SCRIPTURE

"If you love Me,
you will keep My
commandments....
If anyone loves Me,
he will keep My word.
My Father will love
him, and We will come
to him and make Our
home with him."
John 14:15, 23

My wife often reminds me that she wants to hear me say, "I love you." But more than she wants to hear the words, she wants—and deserves—to see the evidence that my words ring true.

It's important that we tell the Lord we love Him through our prayers and praises. But our words of love will be hollow if they're not accompanied by the fruit of obedience. Our love is revealed best through our lifestyle.

How would a more consistent obedience affect my prayer life?

I want my words to match my actions—especially in this:

_____

_____

_____

_____

_____

_____

_____

_____

_____

_____

_____

_____

_____

_____

_____

KINGDOM ACCOUNTABILITY QUESTION:

How am I allowing God's will to be done in my life?

_____

_____

_____

_____

_____

WEEK ONE, DAY FIVE

CHILDLIKE TRUST

SCRIPTURE

"Look at the birds of the sky: they don't sow or reap or gather into barns, yet your heavenly Father feeds them. Aren't you worth more than they?"
Matthew 6:26

Do you ever get anxious about life issues like food and clothing? Do you ever worry that you won't have enough money for basic necessities?

The Father wants us to live anxiety-free lives—the same way children do. They don't experience anxiety, because they trust their parents to provide for all their needs . . . just as our Father has promised to do for us. Why should we not believe He will keep His promise?

How would you express your gratitude for God's provision?

I saw today just how liberating an anxiety-free attitude can be:

_____

_____

_____

_____

_____

_____

_____

_____

_____

_____

_____

_____

_____

_____

KINGDOM ACCOUNTABILITY QUESTION:
How have I experienced God's provision in my life?

_____

_____

_____

_____

_____

EMBRACING THE JOY

SCRIPTURE

You, Lord, are kind and ready to forgive, abundant in faithful love to all who call on You.

Psalm 86:5

We sometimes struggle to accept God's forgiveness because we know better than anyone else the enormity of our sin. But we need to understand the abundance of our Father's love.

If we were to place our sin on one side of the scale and the Lord's loving-kindness on the other, we would rejoice in the truth that the Lord is good and ready to forgive. Our confessed sin is no match for His mercy.

What makes me shy away from seeking God's forgiveness?

_____

_____

_____

_____

_____

_____

_____

_____

Embracing God's forgiveness cleared the way today for me to:

_____

_____

_____

_____

_____

_____

_____

_____

_____

_____

_____

_____

_____

KINGDOM ACCOUNTABILITY QUESTION:
For what do I need forgiveness? Who do I need to forgive?

_____

_____

_____

_____

_____

VICTORIOUS WARRIOR

SCRIPTURE

"The LORD your God is among you, a warrior who saves. He will rejoice over you with gladness. He will quiet you by His love. He will delight in you with shouts of joy."

Zephaniah 3:17

Sometimes we think we are fighting alone. But in our battle with evil, we stand side-by-side with other believers. Even more exciting and powerful than that is the presence of God in our midst—a Victorious Warrior fighting the foe on our behalf.

He will rejoice over us with shouts of joy, with a love for us that runs deep, quiet, and steadfast. Never forget that God is a warrior who is on your side.

What makes me feel so alone in my fight against sin?

_____

_____

_____

_____

_____

_____

_____

_____

I went out today knowing that God was fighting for me, and:

_____

_____

_____

_____

_____

_____

_____

_____

_____

_____

_____

_____

_____

KINGDOM ACCOUNTABILITY QUESTION:

How am I handling temptation? Am I experiencing victory?

_____

_____

_____

_____

_____

·ℰ·

ACCOUNTABILITY

You've hopefully found a lot to think about in responding to the *Kingdom Accountability Questions* that appear at the end of each day's journal entry. These are questions that logically flow from the various phrases of the Lord's Prayer—questions to keep asking yourself in the midst of your own prayer time with the Father. Let's look at each one briefly:

1) *How is my life bringing honor to the Father's name?*

We have a tendency to beat ourselves up over the things we do that discredit our witness. Some of us have trouble ever hearing the Spirit say to us, "Well done!" It's true that one role of the Holy Spirit is to convict us of *sin,* but another is to convict us of *righteousness*—both of our need for a Savior and our success in letting Christ's nature be formed in us. If an earthly father delights in encouraging his children through praise, don't you think your heavenly Father would do the same? The prayer of Jesus invites us to see where God is working in us—where we're responding with obedience.

2) *How am I bringing reproach on the Father's name?*

Still, we never quite outgrow the need to confess our sins before the Lord and each other. But answering this question shouldn't result in a guilt trip. In owning up to our faults, we are freed to move from rebellion to repentance, to give God a submissive heart in which to hallow His name.

3) *How well am I responding to kingdom opportunities?*

Each day is filled with opportunities to make an impact on other's lives for the kingdom of God. And if we're looking for these opportunities ahead of time, we are able to spot them as they happen and respond to God's anytime call. This is where serving God becomes an exhilarating daily adventure.

4) *How am I allowing God's will to be done in my life?*

This is deeper than simple obedience, more personal than seeking the kingdom. This is the ongoing exercise of letting God's will take precedence over ours, making sure that His idea of what's important in our day overshadows all other considerations for how we spend our time.

5) *How have I experienced God's provision in my life?*

The Father promises that He will give us all we need for each day, but because this often occurs without our noticing it, we miss the blessing of seeing His hand at work and thanking Him for specific instances of His fatherly care. Take stock of what God is doing; then you can't help but sense His love.

6) *For what do I need forgiveness? Who do I need to forgive?*

Distance and bitterness can choke our relationship with God and with others. The Lord's Prayer invites us to receive God's forgiveness and also commands us to be as forgiving of others as God has been of us. Plus, if we have either intentionally or unwittingly offended someone, we should always be the first to admit our mistakes and ask their forgiveness.

7) *How am I handling temptation? Am I experiencing victory?*

We simply need a constant reminder of how deceptive the devil is and how quickly we can find ourselves believing a lie. The more we keep this question from the prayer of Jesus before us, the less time we will spend rehashing our sins and the more time we can enjoy celebrating God's deliverance.

WEEK TWO, DAY ONE

LOVE IN
REAL LIFE

SCRIPTURE

"I give you a new commandment: that you love one another. Just as I have loved you, you should also love one another. By this all people will know that you are My disciples."
John 13:34-35

When we honor our Father's name, we exhibit His character through our lifestyle—a lifestyle of love. Jesus told His disciples that people would know that we are His followers when we love each other.

Love is therefore a defining characteristic of those who have experienced the love of the Father—the One who, out of His own love for us, gave His Son to redeem us from our sins.

How should the Father's love for me show itself in my life?

This is what I noticed today about the Father's love for me:

_____

_____

_____

_____

_____

_____

_____

_____

_____

_____

_____

_____

KINGDOM ACCOUNTABILITY QUESTION:
How is my life bringing honor to the Father's name?

_____

_____

_____

_____

WEEK TWO, DAY TWO

MY GREAT PROVIDER

SCRIPTURE

Abraham named
that place "The LORD
Will Provide," so today
it is said: "It will be
provided on the
LORD's mountain."
Genesis 22:14

In the verses leading up to today's passage, Abraham had been given a covenant child, Isaac. Now God had asked him to place that son on the altar. Abraham obeyed God and discovered—through Isaac's deliverance—that one name of God is *Jehovah-Jireh,* the Lord who provides.

The word *Jireh* means "to see." This name reveals a sovereign God whose "*pre*-vision" leads to His *pro*vision.

Is anxiety clouding my view of Jehovah-Jireh? How? Where?

_____

_____

_____

_____

_____

_____

_____

I have realized today how worry can harm my witness:

_____

_____

_____

_____

_____

_____

_____

_____

_____

_____

_____

_____

_____

Kingdom Accountability Question:

How am I bringing reproach on my Father's name?

_____

_____

_____

_____

_____

WEEK TWO, DAY THREE

JUST A LITTLE SOMETHING

SCRIPTURE

If then there is any encouragement in Christ, if any consolation of love, if any fellowship with the Spirit, if any affection and mercy, fulfill my joy by thinking the same way.

Philippians 2:1-2

Did you ever think of encouragement, consolation, fellowship, affection, and mercy as being kingdom activities? We certainly do when we are on the receiving end, like when someone sends us a note of encouragement on a discouraging day.

But kingdom activities include things like phone calls, kind notes, and visits that bring the light of Christ into someone's world. Be on the lookout for them.

I can think of some simple things to do for Christ:

_____

_____

_____

_____

_____

_____

_____

_____

Today I looked for kingdom opportunities in small things:

_____

_____

_____

_____

_____

_____

_____

_____

_____

_____

_____

_____

_____

_____

KINGDOM ACCOUNTABILITY QUESTION:

How well am I responding to kingdom opportunities?

_____

_____

_____

_____

_____

FAITHFUL WARNINGS

SCRIPTURE

"I am going to send an Angel before you to protect you on the way and bring you to the place that I have prepared. Be attentive to Him and listen to His voice."

Exodus 23:20-21

Some of my worst injuries in childhood occurred when I disobeyed my dad. He would warn me not to climb up our fence or something, afraid that I might get hurt if I were to fall. But the times when he turned his back and I ignored his command, my disobedience often resulted in personal pain.

God wants to protect us from the pain of disobedience so that we can truly enjoy His presence.

God has protected me over the years from so many things:

I was thinking today about what disobedience really costs:

_____

_____

_____

_____

_____

_____

_____

_____

_____

_____

_____

_____

KINGDOM ACCOUNTABILITY QUESTION:

How am I allowing God's will to be done in my life?

_____

_____

_____

_____

_____

WEEK TWO, DAY FIVE

SAFE IN
HIS HANDS

SCRIPTURE

"Can any of you add
a single cubit to his
height by worrying?"
Matthew 6:27

Anxiety cannot add a single moment to our lives. If anything, anxiety may well shorten our life span.

Jesus wanted us to understand that our lives are in His Father's hands—a Father who is completely trustworthy, completely loving, completely in control. I cannot think of anything more comforting than knowing that my heavenly Father is looking after my life issues on a daily basis.

Where has anxiety threatened my trust in God's care?

God gave me good reason for not getting worried today:

_____

_____

_____

_____

_____

_____

_____

_____

_____

_____

_____

_____

_____

_____

_____

KINGDOM ACCOUNTABILITY QUESTION:

How have I experienced God's provision in my life?

_____

_____

_____

_____

WEEK TWO, DAY SIX

GETTING OVER IT

SCRIPTURE

Accepting one another and forgiving one another if anyone has a complaint against another. Just as the Lord has forgiven you, so also you must forgive.
Colossians 3:13

Living in Christian community is always a challenge. This is simply a statement of fact. We rub each other the wrong way. We get on each others' nerves. We hurt one another's feelings. The only solution is forgiveness.

Forgiveness allows us to bear with one another. When we know we need to forgive a friend, a family member, or someone at church, we should remember how the Lord has forgiven us.

When do I struggle to forgive and get past the problem?

I told someone today that I was sorry, that I forgave them:

_____

_____

_____

_____

_____

_____

_____

_____

_____

_____

_____

_____

_____

_____

KINGDOM ACCOUNTABILITY QUESTION:

For what do I need forgiveness? Who do I need to forgive?

_____

_____

_____

_____

WEEK TWO, DAY SEVEN

DEVOTED TO RIGHTEOUSNESS

SCRIPTURE

Do not offer any parts of [your body] to sin as weapons for unrighteousness. But as those who are alive from the dead, offer yourselves to God.

Romans 6:13

One of the causes of spiritual defeat is our captivation with sin. It's not an easy choice, but it is a simple one: choosing not to keep offering ourselves to sin.

This choice is not so much about refraining from something; it is about committing ourselves to Christ, about using our lives to praise and proclaim Him, not to gossip, gripe, or pass along crude jokes. By presenting ourselves to God, we shove sin out of the picture.

What is my real struggle: to avoid sin or to submit to Christ?

_____

_____

_____

_____

_____

_____

_____

_____

I learned something today by committing myself to God:

_____

_____

_____

_____

_____

_____

_____

_____

_____

_____

_____

_____

_____

_____

KINGDOM ACCOUNTABILITY QUESTION:

How am I handling temptation? Am I experiencing victory?

_____

_____

_____

_____

_____

THE VALUE OF

⸎

JOURNALING

Some of you are old hands at journaling. For others, this may be the first attempt you've ever made to chronicle your daily spiritual journey. I hope you have found it to be a rewarding experience.

No doubt you have found that on some days your thoughts flow more freely than on others. This is natural. Each day is a little different, and though we should never let other things preoccupy our attention from spiritual matters, we needn't expect walking with God to be mechanical and predictable.

You have also probably had days when it was difficult to find even the brief moments required to journal your thoughts. Don't get discouraged by this or give up. One benefit gained from the process of journaling is developing the discipline of writing about spiritual realities daily. So if you get behind, just jump back in. Or do two days' worth at once. Stick with this program, and you will find that it yields worthwhile results. Keep some of these thoughts in mind:

1) *Watch for patterns in what God is saying.*

As you look back over the notes you've been writing in the previous weeks, you may notice certain trends beginning to develop in your thinking.

• Are you seeing any patterns?

• Are there certain questions that are more difficult to answer?

• Why do you think that would be the case?

• Have you found that this journaling discipline has made you think more intentionally about the commitments you have made to the Lord and about His provision for you?

2) *Notice what God is doing with your confessed sin.*

You may have seen that the way you confess the sin in your life is changing. Some of the struggles you have had in the past are becoming easier to deal with. Or perhaps God is testing your faith by continuing to allow familiar temptations to heat up, but you've chosen to lean hard on His power to deliver you, and you're experiencing exciting spiritual victories. Merely becoming more sensitive to our Father's name gives us a solid, compelling reason for avoiding habitual, sinful activities. This is a wonderful discovery, because then we don't have to go through that awful pattern of repeated sin, the discouragement of our own failures and their unnecessary consequences. The Father wants you to know His abundance. Even in a "nobody's perfect" world, you—yes, you!—can walk in consistent purity and holiness. No one has a fuller, richer life than believers who are walking in victory!

3) *Be sure to keep track of God's kingdom activity.*

As you pray through the pages on kingdom activity, are you becoming more aware of what God is doing around you each day? Seeing God's kingdom activity is a matter of knowing what to look for. A trained bird watcher can spot a particular bird quickly, while a novice will struggle. But when the veteran watcher shows you what to look for, you can begin seeing the same scenes with new attentiveness. With practice, your eyes quickly focus on the object of your desire. Jesus told us how He did this: "For the Father loves the Son and shows Him everything He is doing" (John 5:20). He will show us, too.

WEEK THREE, DAY ONE

LOVE FOR THE FATHERLESS

SCRIPTURE

Look at how great
a love the Father has
given us, that we should
be called God's children.
And we are! The reason
the world does not
know us is that it
didn't know Him.
1 John 3:1

Nothing touches my heart deeper than the needs of my children. The mere sound of their voice moves me to action. In the same way, our Father's desire is to show us His great love.

But others do not always understand this vital relationship of ours, and they often react negatively to it. Yet we honor our Father's name by showing them kindness, even when they give us the opposite in return.

How can I honor God's name around those who resent it?

_____

_____

_____

_____

_____

_____

_____

_____

I had a chance today to love someone who's hard to love:

_____

_____

_____

_____

_____

_____

_____

_____

_____

_____

_____

_____

_____

_____

_____

KINGDOM ACCOUNTABILITY QUESTION:

How is my life bringing honor to the Father's name?

_____

_____

_____

_____

_____

WEEK THREE, DAY TWO

THE JOY OF BELIEVING

SCRIPTURE

We wait for the LORD;
He is our help and
shield. For our hearts
rejoice in Him,
because we trust
in His holy name.
Psalm 33:20-21

The words *joy* and *rejoice* are found throughout the Bible. They are the peaceful reward of those who know the Father firsthand, who trust in His daily provision and abiding presence.

Every one of us faces difficult situations in life. But joy is that deep stream of peace that flows unseen beneath the turbulence of everyday circumstances. Our joy speaks volumes about the powerful name of the God we serve.

In what areas of my life have I lost the joy of trusting God?

_____

_____

_____

_____

_____

_____

_____

_____

Today I saw how my joy (or the lack of it) speaks to people:

_____

_____

_____

_____

_____

_____

_____

_____

_____

_____

_____

_____

_____

_____

KINGDOM ACCOUNTABILITY QUESTION:

How am I bringing reproach on my Father's name?

_____

_____

_____

_____

_____

GO SERVE SOMEBODY

SCRIPTURE

"If I, your Lord and Teacher, have washed your feet, you also ought to wash one another's feet. For I have given you an example that you also should do just as I have done for you."
John 13:14-15

Jesus had gathered His disciples for the final Passover before His death. A basin and towel had been prepared for the cleansing of the guests' feet. But no servant was available to take care of this menial duty.

The disciples all sidestepped the basin, assuming someone else would stoop and serve. And Someone did! Jesus washed their feet! Even a lowly task done in Christ's name is kingdom activity.

Where is pride getting in the way of my service to Christ?

God showed me an opportunity today to serve someone:

_____

_____

_____

_____

_____

_____

_____

_____

_____

_____

_____

_____

_____

KINGDOM ACCOUNTABILITY QUESTION:

How well am I responding to kingdom opportunities?

_____

_____

_____

_____

_____

WEEK THREE, DAY FOUR

ALIVE ON
THE VINE

SCRIPTURE

"I am the vine; you are the branches. The one who remains in Me and I in him produces much fruit.... If you remain in Me and My words remain in you, ask whatever you want and it will be done for you."
John 15:5,7

These verses contain one of the most cherished prayer promises in all of the Scriptures, as well as one of its most neglected commands.

Jesus tells us to abide in Him. If we disobey this command, we inevitably decay into fruitlessness. But when we stay connected to the vine through prayer and intimacy with Christ, fruit begins to grow and our desires begin lining up naturally with God's will.

What does "abiding in Christ" really look like in my life?

_____

_____

_____

_____

_____

_____

_____

_____

This is what I experienced today by abiding in the Vine:

_____
_____
_____
_____
_____
_____
_____
_____
_____
_____
_____
_____
_____
_____
_____

KINGDOM ACCOUNTABILITY QUESTION:
How am I allowing God's will to be done in my life?

_____
_____
_____
_____
_____

WEEK THREE, DAY FIVE

WHAT AM I SO WORRIED ABOUT?

SCRIPTURE

"Don't worry about tomorrow, because tomorrow will worry about itself. Each day has enough trouble of its own."
Matthew 6:34

How much time do you waste in worrying about tomorrow? We know from experience that in a majority of cases, the actual events are much more benign than all the possible disasters we imagined.

We then wonder, "Why did I spend so much energy agonizing for nothing?" When we trust God for our daily bread, we recognize that His provision will be sufficient for each day as it occurs.

What have I gained as a result of all my worrying?

_____

_____

_____

_____

_____

_____

_____

_____

I've been worried a lot lately, but today I began letting it go:

_____

_____

_____

_____

_____

_____

_____

_____

_____

_____

_____

_____

_____

_____

KINGDOM ACCOUNTABILITY QUESTION:

How have I experienced God's provision in my life?

_____

_____

_____

_____

_____

WEEK THREE, DAY SIX

WHITER THAN SNOW

SCRIPTURE

"Come, let us discuss this," says the LORD. "Though your sins are like scarlet, they will be as white as snow; though they are as red as crimson, they will be like wool."
Isaiah 1:18

I love waking up to a covering of fresh snowfall—a wet, heavy snow that clings to trees and accumulates in the yard. It places a blanket of beauty over everything, making even an unsightly landscape appear clean and white.

When we confess our sins to God, He blankets them with His forgiveness. No longer is their grime exposed to His view, but He sees us covered in His love—pure and holy in His sight.

What does God's blanket of forgiveness mean to me?

_____

_____

_____

_____

_____

_____

_____

_____

The totality of God's forgiveness really hit me today:

_____

_____

_____

_____

_____

_____

_____

_____

_____

_____

_____

_____

_____

KINGDOM ACCOUNTABILITY QUESTION:

For what do I need forgiveness? Who do I need to forgive?

_____

_____

_____

_____

_____

FAITH IN HIS FAITHFULNESS

SCRIPTURE

We may be delivered from wicked and evil men, for not all have faith. But the Lord is faithful; He will strengthen and guard you from the evil one.

2 Thessalonians 3:2-3

Our victory over evil is dependent on the faithfulness of the Lord, not on our own meager faithfulness. God is trustworthy by His very nature; He will not abandon us in the midst of our struggle but will strengthen and protect us from the evil one!

God has taken the responsibility on Himself for delivering us from evil. We are merely responsible for submitting our way to His protection and power.

How am I relying on God's power to deliver me from evil?

_____

_____

_____

_____

_____

_____

_____

_____

My faithful Lord provided me a way of escape today:

_____

_____

_____

_____

_____

_____

_____

_____

_____

_____

_____

_____

_____

_____

KINGDOM ACCOUNTABILITY QUESTION:

How am I handling temptation? Am I experiencing victory?

_____

_____

_____

_____

ACCESS TO GOD

I don't think most of us grasp the absolute wonder of being able to address God as Father. If we did, we wouldn't treat prayer as an optional exercise or enter lightly into His presence. This One who has given us permission to address Him with the tender, familial term of "Father" is the creator of the entire universe. Even Jesus, the unique Son of God, treasured the significance of this heavenly relationship, much to the shock and disbelief of His opponents.

1) *Access to the Father in Jesus' life.*

In John 5 we find the story of Jesus healing a man on the Sabbath, which raised the ire and indignation of His contemporaries. But in response to their taunts and persecution, He gave this simple explanation for His actions: "My Father is still working, and I also am working." (v. 17).

Verse 18 describes the reaction this statement drew: "This is why the Jews began trying all the more to kill Him: not only was He breaking the Sabbath, but He was even calling God His own Father, making Himself equal with God." ·

Jesus' response to this threat was equally simple and direct, saying that "the Son is not able to do anything on His own, but only what He sees the Father doing. For whatever the Father does, these things the Son also does in the same way" (v. 19).

Over and over in the Gospels, we see Jesus in fellowship with His Father, never making a move without the Father's leading, going to Him before sunrise or throughout an all-night vigil, hanging on every word, walking in perfect fellowship. Read the accounts of Christ's life, and you see a Father and Son who are inseparable. Can we, then, possibly live for Him on our own?

2) *Access to the Father in our lives.*

In my den at home, I have a picture taken with George Bush, the 41st President, as well as one with his son, the 43rd President. I am proud of both pictures. Truth is, though, I don't actually "know" either of them, and they would have no reason to know me. I just happened to be in the right place at the right time. Perhaps you have a picture of yourself with a celebrity or sports hero. Perhaps you're even on a first-name basis with a famous or influential person. We are inclined to think that our proximity or relationship with someone of that stature gives us a certain measure of esteem and value. We like having access to powerful people.

But nothing should rival the significance of having daily, constant access to our heavenly Father, the creator and sustainer of all things. Because of our personal relationship with the Son, we can address God as "Father" and have constant access to Him. Further, He has promised to show us what He is doing in the world around us because He loves us. This thought not only creates a sense of awe in me but a desire to communicate with my "Dad" throughout the day.

3) *Access to the Father for all believers, for all time.*

We can hear the same sense of awe in Paul's voice. "For this reason I bow my knees before the Father from whom every family in heaven and on earth is named" (Ephesians 3:14-15). All who trust in Christ for salvation can pray to the Father of all, the creator of the universe, the Lord of all, and can call Him "Father." What more could any mortal ask for? Tell someone today about this glorious privilege.

WEEK FOUR, DAY ONE

EXPRESSIONS OF HIS LOVE

SCRIPTURE

We are not obligated to the flesh to live according to the flesh. . . . All those led by God's Spirit are God's sons.

Romans 8:12,14

Children reflect the character of their father; they follow his leadership. What then does it mean to be led by the Spirit of God, to follow in the footsteps of our Father?

The Spirit's purpose is to bear witness to Christ. So we who are led by the Spirit should be developing unselfish goals and priorities that point to and glorify Christ. We should be living the Father's love everywhere we go.

How am I handling opportunities to tell others about Christ?

I talked with someone today who needs the Father's love:

_____
_____
_____
_____
_____
_____
_____
_____
_____
_____
_____
_____
_____
_____

KINGDOM ACCOUNTABILITY QUESTION:

How is my life bringing honor to the Father's name?

_____
_____
_____
_____

FOR HIS NAME'S SAKE

SCRIPTURE

The LORD is my shepherd; there is nothing I lack. He lets me lie down in green pastures; He leads me beside quiet waters. He renews my life; He leads me along the right paths for His name's sake.

Psalm 23:1-3

Perhaps no passage in Scripture is as beloved as Psalm 23. "The LORD is my shepherd" translates the name *Jehovah Rohi*. Read the entire Psalm and remind yourself of all that the Father has promised to do for you.

Jesus referred to Himself as the Good Shepherd (John 10:11). He declared that His sheep hear and obey His voice. By consistently obeying what He says, we bring honor to the name of God.

What has God been saying to me lately about obedience?

_____

_____

_____

_____

_____

_____

_____

_____

I'm starting to see why obedience is "for His name's sake":

_____

_____

_____

_____

_____

_____

_____

_____

_____

_____

_____

_____

_____

_____

_____

KINGDOM ACCOUNTABILITY QUESTION:
How am I bringing reproach on my Father's name?

_____

_____

_____

_____

AT HOME IN THE KINGDOM

SCRIPTURE

"If two of you on earth agree about any matter that you pray for, it will be done for you by My Father in heaven. For where two or three are gathered together in My name, I am there among them."
Matthew 18:19-20

There is incredible power in the gathered community of believers. While the Lord is always with us, He has chosen to manifest Himself in great power when His children gather in His name.

Yes, we should participate in God's kingdom activity in every arena of life, but we shouldn't neglect the opportunities He provides us through the life of our church. God is always at work somewhere in the midst of His people.

Where do I see kingdom activity occurring in my church?

_____

_____

_____

_____

_____

_____

_____

A few fellow believers and I got together recently and:

_____

_____

_____

_____

_____

_____

_____

_____

_____

_____

_____

_____

_____

_____

KINGDOM ACCOUNTABILITY QUESTION:

How well am I responding to kingdom opportunities?

_____

_____

_____

_____

WEEK FOUR, DAY FOUR

SHOW ME WHAT TO DO

SCRIPTURE

"I do not call you slaves anymore, because a slave doesn't know what his master is doing. I have called you friends, because I have made known to you everything I have heard from My Father."
John 15:15

Because of our relationship with the Father through the Son, we are now God's friends. One of the benefits of our friendship is the promise that Jesus will always make known to us everything He has heard from the Father.

So if we want to do the will of God, if we are serious about seeking His kingdom activity through the day, we can do so with the full assurance that Christ will reveal it to us.

How does God reveal what His will for me is?

It wasn't what I felt like doing, but I knew it was God's will:

_____

_____

_____

_____

_____

_____

_____

_____

_____

_____

_____

_____

_____

_____

KINGDOM ACCOUNTABILITY QUESTION:

How am I allowing God's will to be done in my life?

_____

_____

_____

_____

_____

ALL DAY,
ALL NIGHT

SCRIPTURE

The LORD will send
His faithful love by day;
His song will be with
me in the night—
a prayer to the God
of my life.

Psalm 42:8

This verse reminds us that God is always with us, embracing us with a love that promises His covenant loyalty. God is always trustworthy.

One of the most precious pictures of early childhood is of a mother singing a lullaby to her infant child, her soothing voice allowing the baby to drift off into a restful sleep. God's love is like that— a near companion in the daytime and a trusted guardian through the night.

What time of day do I tend to worry the most? Why?

Today I leaned on the promises of God's love and loyalty:

_____

_____

_____

_____

_____

_____

_____

_____

_____

_____

_____

_____

_____

_____

KINGDOM ACCOUNTABILITY QUESTION:
How have I experienced God's provision in my life?

_____

_____

_____

_____

_____

FINALLY FED UP

SCRIPTURE

You took away Your people's guilt; You covered all their sin. You withdrew all Your fury; You turned from Your burning anger.
Psalm 85:2-3

God hates sin because sin is destructive to us—men and women who are created in His image. The object of His fury is not us but the sin that seeks to destroy us.

God's desire is to forgive the sin of His people, to cover it with His love and mercy. He wants to deliver us from the wrath He must pour out on sin. Much better than we do, He knows how much sin really costs us.

Am I truly angry about the sins I continue to harbor?

My sins are against God. That truth came home to me today:

_____

_____

_____

_____

_____

_____

_____

_____

_____

_____

_____

_____

_____

_____

_____

_____

KINGDOM ACCOUNTABILITY QUESTION:

For what do I need forgiveness? Who do I need to forgive?

_____

_____

_____

_____

STILL GOING STRONG

SCRIPTURE

Keeping our eyes on Jesus, the source and perfecter of our faith … consider Him who endured such hostility from sinners against Himself, so that you won't grow weary and lose heart.
Hebrews 12:2,3

All of my football coaches in high school and college believed in rigorous physical conditioning, always reminding us that most games were lost in the fourth quarter, when fatigue took over.

We have a Champion who has already completed the course and has sat down victoriously at the right hand of the throne of God. When we keep our focus on Him, we will not grow weary in our battle against evil.

When do I tend to flag and falter in my obedience to God?

_____

_____

_____

_____

_____

_____

_____

_____

I was spiritually out of gas today, but God filled me up:

_____

_____

_____

_____

_____

_____

_____

_____

_____

_____

_____

_____

_____

_____

KINGDOM ACCOUNTABILITY QUESTION:

How am I handling temptation? Am I experiencing victory?

_____

_____

_____

_____

_____

In the same way that you've been discovering new things along the way in this journal, I can honestly tell you that I have learned more about the Lord's Prayer after writing *The Prayer of Jesus* book than while I was actually working on it. Asking the Father to make me sensitive to His kingdom activity has made me more patient, less anxious, and more aware of what He is doing around me in the lives of others.

More than anything, I have a renewed desire to tell others the goodness of the gospel. Like most people, I sometimes find it difficult to engage people in evangelistic conversations. I feel like the tongue-tied teenager trying to ask out his beloved for their first date. But when I allow the Father to open the door to witnessing—rather than my trying to force it open—the whole process flows much more naturally.

1) *Case in point.*

The other day I was on a full plane, wedged onto a single row of seats with two other guys about my size. I began breathing my commitments: *Make me aware that I bear Your name; help me to see Your kingdom activity, and allow me to participate.* I struck up a conversation with the gentleman beside me. He was cordial but unresponsive to any attempt I made to engage him in spiritual matters. My frustration grew as I tried to pry the door open. Finally, though, I relaxed and breathed another prayer: *Dad, I'm not getting anywhere, but I am still willing to do whatever You ask. I'll leave this in Your hands.* I proceeded to take a short nap. (I guess Dad knew I was tired.) The stewardess soon woke me up with her serving cart. I accepted a cup of hot coffee, then I got out several unfinished pages from this journal. My seatmate looked at the notes and asked me if I was working on a sermon. "No," I told him, "I'm putting together a prayer journal." In a few moments we were engaged in a very natural conversation that allowed me to easily present the gospel.

2) *Another true story.*

Not long ago I was headed from Dallas to a meeting in Nashville. When I arrived at the airport check-in counter, I discovered that my plane was delayed. And you know what my first reaction was? To smile. Living in the Lord's Prayer makes life an adventure. You just can't get worked up about it.

I asked at the desk to see if they would make an announcement in the Admiral's Club when the plane was ready to leave. As I began to head in the direction of the club, I encountered an anxious businessman and invited him to join me there. He accepted my invitation. On the way the man told me that he was going to Nashville because he had just purchased a new business, and he was anxious to get on the way. I told him that our anxiety served no good purpose. He wanted to know if it was really possible to live anxiety-free. I then told him more about the prayer of Jesus and the Father's care for us. He commented that he wasn't surprised that Jesus could live without anxiety since He was the Father's Son. I then assured him that this was the point of the invitation to pray "our Father."

I knew then that even if I missed my Nashville meeting, this kingdom moment had made the trip to the airport a wise investment of the Father's time.

And that's how it works, with ordinary folks like you and me, every time we just get in the car and let God do the driving.

WEEK FIVE, DAY ONE

HELD IN HIS HAND

SCRIPTURE

"I, the LORD, have called you in righteousness, and I will hold you by your hand; I will keep you, and I will make you a covenant for the people, a light for the nations."

Isaiah 42:6

When we who bear the Father's name reflect His righteous character, He enables us to be a light to others.

What an honor to be appointed by God as a bearer of His light—light which exposes the darkness for what it is and provides guidance to those who have lost their way in it. It's a difficult task, but the Father promises to hold us by the hand and watch over us, to keep us strong as we hold high His light.

How can I be a light to someone lost in the darkness?

_____

_____

_____

_____

_____

_____

_____

_____

I trusted God today to help me shine His light in my world:

_____

_____

_____

_____

_____

_____

_____

_____

_____

_____

_____

_____

KINGDOM ACCOUNTABILITY QUESTION:

How is my life bringing honor to the Father's name?

_____

_____

_____

_____

_____

WEEK FIVE, DAY TWO

UNDER
HIS FLAG

SCRIPTURE

Moses built an altar and named it, "The LORD Is My Banner." He said, "Indeed, my hand is lifted up toward the LORD's throne! The LORD will be at war with Amalek from generation to generation."
Exodus 17:15-16

Israel—recently freed from Egyptian bondage—was no match militarily for the warlike Amalekites. But God commanded Moses to go to the top of the mountain and lift his staff aloft. As long as they fought under the banner of the Lord's rod, Israel was victorious.

Israel learned that day that God was *Jehovah-Nissi,* their banner of victory. We honor His name every time we let Him fight the battles in our lives.

Where do I most commonly lose my spiritual battles?

_____

_____

_____

_____

_____

_____

_____

_____

Today I let God do the fighting. Here's how it turned out:

_____

_____

_____

_____

_____

_____

_____

_____

_____

_____

_____

_____

_____

_____

KINGDOM ACCOUNTABILITY QUESTION:

How am I bringing reproach on my Father's name?

_____

_____

_____

_____

_____

WEEK FIVE, DAY THREE

SERVICE WITH A SMILE

SCRIPTURE

"Whoever wants to become great among you must be your servant, and whoever wants to be first among you must be a slave to all. For even the Son of Man did not come to be served."
Mark 10:43-45

Sometimes we do not participate in kingdom service because we are waiting to see the Red Sea opened or the walls of Jericho fall. We forget that God's kingdom activity can be found even in humble acts of service.

Take the opportunity to seek God's kingdom today simply by putting others needs before your own. These events often happen close to home. Always be watching for the Father's activity.

What does kingdom activity look like in my own home?

_____

_____

_____

_____

_____

_____

_____

_____

I found God's work today by doing something as basic as:

_____

_____

_____

_____

_____

_____

_____

_____

_____

_____

_____

_____

_____

_____

_____

KINGDOM ACCOUNTABILITY QUESTION:

How well am I responding to kingdom opportunities?

_____

_____

_____

_____

_____

WEEK FIVE, DAY FOUR

HE CAN BE TRUSTED

SCRIPTURE

"Father, if You are willing, take this cup away from Me— nevertheless, not My will, but Yours, be done."
Luke 22:42

We are all familiar with this agonized but obedient prayer of the Son as He faced death on the cross. The agony was not so much for the cruel form of death He faced, but for the weight of sin He had chosen to bear. He who knew no sin became the sin offering for us.

Why? Obedience to the Father. Jesus knew that His Father was totally trustworthy. Our obedience, too, springs from our confidence in our Father.

In what ways has God shown Himself trustworthy to me?

_____

_____

_____

_____

_____

_____

_____

_____

Today I did something based solely on God's promises:

_____

_____

_____

_____

_____

_____

_____

_____

_____

_____

_____

_____

_____

_____

_____

KINGDOM ACCOUNTABILITY QUESTION:

How am I allowing God's will to be done in my life?

_____

_____

_____

_____

_____

WEEK FIVE, DAY FIVE

BEYOND BELIEF

SCRIPTURE

Don't worry about anything, but in everything, through prayer and petition with thanksgiving, let your requests be made known to God. And the peace of God ... will guard your hearts and your minds.
Philippians 4:6-7

One of the greatest testimonies to God's presence on earth is the peace exhibited by His followers in the midst of life's storms. Paul tells us we have only two options: worry or prayer.

Spend some time letting this verse transformed from words on a page to faith in God's constant provision. Then thank Him for His faithfulness and for all of His past provision. The peace of God defies any other explanation.

The Father will never fail me. How does that make me feel?

_____

_____

_____

_____

_____

_____

_____

_____

I was looking for God's peace today, and He gave it to me:

_____

_____

_____

_____

_____

_____

_____

_____

_____

_____

_____

_____

_____

KINGDOM ACCOUNTABILITY QUESTION:
How have I experienced God's provision in my life?

_____

_____

_____

_____

BURNING
THE NOTE

SCRIPTURE

When you were dead in trespasses and in the uncircumcision of your flesh, He made you alive with Him and forgave us all our trespasses. He erased the certificate of debt, with its obligations.

Colossians 2:13-14

My dad was my pastor when I was growing up. I can still see his broad grin as he stood in the pulpit with a flaming piece of paper clutched in his fingers, burning the note which signified that all the debt on our church building had been paid.

When Jesus died on the cross, He paid the sin debt for all believers. All the penalties we owed were taken out of the way. Faith has won our forgiveness.

What causes me to live out of step with this reality?

_____

_____

_____

_____

_____

_____

_____

_____

I had a chance to share today about God's full forgiveness:

_____

_____

_____

_____

_____

_____

_____

_____

_____

_____

_____

_____

_____

KINGDOM ACCOUNTABILITY QUESTION:

For what do I need forgiveness? Who do I need to forgive?

_____

_____

_____

_____

OUT IN THE OPEN

SCRIPTURE

If we walk in the light as He Himself is in the light, we have fellowship with one another, and the blood of Jesus His Son cleanses us from all sin.
1 John 1:7

Where there are dark areas in our home and life—places that cloak the evil in our hearts—we must put safety lights in place to dispel the darkness and experience two great realities:

1) Fellowship with other Christians. There is safety in numbers. We stand against evil by maintaining good relationships with our Christian family.

2) The cleansing blood of Jesus—the only freedom this world has to offer.

What dark places do I find myself too comfortable living in?

_____

_____

_____

_____

_____

_____

_____

_____

I stayed in the light all day today, and here's what I found:

_____

_____

_____

_____

_____

_____

_____

_____

_____

_____

_____

_____

_____

_____

_____

KINGDOM ACCOUNTABILITY QUESTION:

How am I handling temptation? Am I experiencing victory?

_____

_____

_____

_____

Father

If we are going to pray the Lord's Prayer with the absolute abandon that Jesus prayed it, we must know our Father's nature so that we can fully trust Him. My prayer life has been greatly enhanced by an understanding of my Father's attributes.

1) *The Father knows everything.*

Bible teachers refer to this attribute as *omniscience.* I am not as moved by the fact that God knows *everything* as I am by the truth that He knows everything about *me*—and still loves me. He knows every pain I feel, every discouragement I experience, every flaw in my character, every hidden fear. Yet He chooses to welcome me into His presence; He promises to meet my every need. When you know that your Father knows everything about you and still loves you, it adds freedom to your prayer life and a sense of security throughout the day.

2) *The Father is everywhere.*

I find it comforting to know that my Father is always present, or *omnipresent.* There is nowhere that I will go this week and nothing that I will encounter this afternoon that can separate me from the presence of my Father. Do you remember the confidence of David who declared that he would not be afraid even if he were to walk through the valley of the shadow of death? How could he possibly say that? He knew that God would be with him. David expresses this truth in Psalm 139: "Where can I go to escape Your Spirit? Where can I flee from Your presence? If I go up to heaven, You are there; if I make my bed in Sheol, You are there. If I live at the eastern horizon or settle at the western limits, even there Your hand will lead me; Your right hand will hold on to me." (vv. 7-10).

3) *The Father can do anything.*

Our Father has all power; He is *omnipotent*. There are many references to this truth throughout the Bible, but none are any clearer than Psalm 115:3, where the writer compares the lifeless idols of the day with the one true God who "is in heaven and does whatever He pleases." How awesome to know that our heavenly Father, with all authority in heaven and on earth, guides our every step. He possesses no limitations, for He has all power. We can depend on Him with full assurance throughout every moment of every day.

4) *The Father is altogether good.*

He is not only all-knowing, all-powerful, and always with us, He is altogether good and righteous—*omni-benevolent*. The Psalmist declared: "God, within Your temple, we contemplate Your faithful love. Your name, God, like Your praise, reaches to the ends of the earth; Your right hand is filled with justice" (Psalm 48:9-10). Jesus underlines this truth when He compares our prayer with that of a son's request to his earthly father, who would certainly not give his son a stone when he requested bread, or give a snake when asked for a fish. "If you then, who are evil, know how to give good gifts to your children, how much more will your Father in heaven give good things to those who ask Him!" (Matthew 7:11). It is contrary to the Father's character to do evil to His children.

Our Father knows us, He cares for us, He is always with us, He has all power, and He is altogether good. And wonder of wonders, He invites us to spend our day in His presence. Prayer is simply constant communion with our Dad.

ALL DAY PRAISE

SCRIPTURE

It is good to praise the LORD, to sing praise to Your name, Most High, to declare Your faithful love in the morning and Your faithfulness at night.

Psalm 92:1-2

We have focused a lot on honoring the Father's name. One of the greatest ways we can do that is by giving thanks and singing praises to His name.

This happens, of course, when we gather with other believers to worship. But thanksgiving and praise should be a natural part of our daily conversations with the Father. What moves the heart of a father more than the gratitude of his children?

How can I make worship a more significant part of my day?

_____

_____

_____

_____

_____

_____

_____

_____

Here's what the Father taught me today about praise:

_____

_____

_____

_____

_____

_____

_____

_____

_____

_____

_____

_____

_____

_____

KINGDOM ACCOUNTABILITY QUESTION:
How is my life bringing honor to the Father's name?

_____

_____

_____

_____

_____

WEEK SIX, DAY TWO

HERE, THERE, AND EVERYWHERE

SCRIPTURE

"Its perimeter will be six miles, and from that day the name of the city will be 'The LORD Is There.' "
Ezekiel 48:35

Israel grew to identify God's presence with the temple. But in the period when Ezekiel wrote, the temple lay in ruins. So how could Israel know and experience God's presence *then*?

The prophet tells of a new temple, situated in a city known by a simple yet powerful name: "The LORD is there"— *Jehovah Shammah*. When you feel alone, distant from God, remind yourself that the Father is always with you.

When God seems far away, how can I sense His presence?

_____

_____

_____

_____

_____

_____

_____

_____

God was there for me today:

KINGDOM ACCOUNTABILITY QUESTION:

How am I bringing reproach on my Father's name?

WHAT'S FOUND IN GIVING

SCRIPTURE

The One who provides seed for the sower and bread for food will provide and multiply your seed and increase the harvest of your righteousness, as you are enriched in every way for all generosity.

2 Corinthians 9:10-11

Paul was writing to the Corinthians about the opportunity of sending a relief offering to help other believers suffering from a severe famine. Using an agricultural metaphor, he promised them that just as God provided the seed that resulted in the harvest, the church's gift would yield a great return in ways more valuable than money.

When we give what is precious to us, God is honored through our sacrifice.

Why is giving such an important part of God's kingdom?

_____

_____

_____

_____

_____

_____

_____

_____

I thought today about some ways I can be a better giver:

_____

_____

_____

_____

_____

_____

_____

_____

_____

_____

_____

_____

_____

_____

KINGDOM ACCOUNTABILITY QUESTION:

How well am I responding to kingdom opportunities?

_____

_____

_____

_____

_____

GIVING IT YOUR ALL

SCRIPTURE

Brothers, by the mercies of God, I urge you to present your bodies as a living sacrifice, holy and pleasing to God; this is your spiritual worship.

Romans 12:1

If we are going to live fruitful Christian lives, we must first present ourselves to God for His service.

This "living sacrifice" lifestyle is not reserved for super-Christians. The Bible says that it is simply a logical conclusion based on our profession of faith in Christ. It is the natural consequence of our confession. As we continually contemplate the depths of His mercy, we find that His will is our sole desire.

Where do I find this "living sacrifice" the hardest to make?

_____

_____

_____

_____

_____

_____

_____

I can state for a fact that living for God makes perfect sense:

_____

_____

_____

_____

_____

_____

_____

_____

_____

_____

_____

_____

_____

_____

KINGDOM ACCOUNTABILITY QUESTION:

How am I allowing God's will to be done in my life?

_____

_____

_____

_____

_____

WEEK SIX, DAY FIVE

ALWAYS ON
THE JOB

SCRIPTURE

"The eyes of the
LORD range to and fro
throughout the earth
to show Himself strong
for those whose heart
is at perfect peace
with Him."
2 Chronicles 16:9

The image in this verse is profoundly comforting. God is vigilantly looking throughout the earth with the purpose of strongly supporting those—like us—whose hearts are completely His.

Yesterday we focused on obedience in our commitment to the Lord. Notice that this complete surrender to the Father's will is rewarded by His love and care. There is nothing skimpy about God's provision for our daily needs.

What is God's purpose in going to such lengths of love?

No one but God could have done what He did today:

KINGDOM ACCOUNTABILITY QUESTION:
How have I experienced God's provision in my life?

NOT GUILTY

SCRIPTURE

If anyone does sin, we have an advocate with the Father—Jesus Christ the righteous One. He Himself is the propitiation for our sins, and not only for ours, but also for those of the whole world.

1 John 2:1-2

When we understand that our sin grieves the Spirit, we will want to avoid sin. But when we do sin, we know we have an Advocate with the Father.

The language is from the courtroom. We have a lawyer to plead our case: Jesus Christ, the righteous One, who steps before the Father in our defense. When we keep this picture in our minds, it gives us great confidence as we daily confess our sins.

Do I realize how free I really am from sin's hold on me?

When I confessed my sins to God today, it made me feel like:

_____

_____

_____

_____

_____

_____

_____

_____

_____

_____

_____

_____

_____

KINGDOM ACCOUNTABILITY QUESTION:

For what do I need forgiveness? Who do I need to forgive?

_____

_____

_____

_____

INNER STRENGTH

SCRIPTURE

You are from God, little children, and you have conquered them, because the One who is in you is greater than the one who is in the world.

1 John 4:4

We are not called to withstand the daily, accumulating pressures of temptation in our own strength. Instead we have been given the indwelling power of the Holy Spirit to live in us . . . and this glorious declaration from heaven's throne: "the One who is in you is greater than the one who is in the world."

So take that, Satan! We have fallen for your lies before, but we stand today in the strength of Almighty God!

What does trusting God's deliverance require of me?

God's power turned me into a tower of strength today:

_____

_____

_____

_____

_____

_____

_____

_____

_____

_____

_____

_____

_____

_____

KINGDOM ACCOUNTABILITY QUESTION:

How am I handling temptation? Am I experiencing victory?

_____

_____

_____

_____

_____

Anxiety

Have you ever noticed how small children do not exhibit anxiety like we adults do? They don't spend unnecessary time worrying about how they are going to pay for food. It just "magically appears on the table," as far as the child is concerned. They aren't anxious about their physical safety or their daily needs unless we adults project our anxiety onto them. They don't lie awake at night worrying about the mounting bills.

Don't you wish you could live with a worry-free, childlike attitude like that? Good news: that's the kind of lifestyle Jesus demonstrated in His childlike dependence on the Father—the kind of life He invites us to experience as we join Him in praying to "our Father." Is it any surprise, then, that the verses which follow the Lord's Prayer (Matthew 6:25-34) include repeated references to our not being anxious?

1) *Food*.

• "I tell you: Don't worry about your life, what you will eat,"

2) *Necessities*.

• "Or what you will drink,"

3) *Clothing*.

• "Or about your body, what you will wear. Isn't life more than food and the body more than clothing?"

4) *Today*.

• "Can any of you add a single cubit to his height by worrying?"

5) *Tomorrow*.

• "Therefore don't worry about tomorrow, because tomorrow will worry about itself. Each day has enough trouble of its own."

Five times in the span of ten verses. And each time, He uses an imperative term that literally amounts to a *commandment* not to worry—a heavenly ban on anxiety.

Do you remember when the disciples asked Jesus about who would be the greatest in the kingdom of heaven? He gave the disciples an object lesson they would never forget. He set a child before them and declared: "I assure you . . . unless you are converted and become like children, you will never enter the kingdom of heaven. Therefore, whoever humbles himself like this child—this one is the greatest in the kingdom of heaven." (Matthew 18:3-4). A child who is totally dependent on his father has no pretenses, no worries. And no wonder: his Father has his needs totally covered!

Jesus has invited each of us who believe in Him to live in this kind of trusting, dynamic relationship with our Father, to declare a ban on anxiety, and to walk in the confidence of met needs, for our Father has promised to provide. So . . .

1) *Pray.*

• Talk with your Father about every incident of your day.

2) *Read the Word.*

• Get His perspective on everything you experience.

3) *Listen.*

• Ask Him how you can live in such a way that you honor His name, advance His kingdom, and do His will.

4) *Get out there and live it.*

• Relax in the knowledge that He will provide daily bread, forgiveness, and victory over evil.

WEEK SEVEN, DAY ONE

A GODLY HERITAGE

SCRIPTURE

Not to us, LORD, not to us, but to Your name give glory because of Your faithful love, because of Your truth.

Psalm 115:1

My dad had a great interest in our family name. He would order books that chronicled the exploits of those who bore the name "Hemphill."

I am proud of the heritage that has been passed on to me through my earthly father's name, but my greatest priority is to give glory to my heavenly Father's name, to reveal His love and His truth to everyone I meet. Only His name has the power to save.

Name some benefits of the Father's lovingkindness and truth:

Here's how I experienced the Father's love in my life today:

_____

_____

_____

_____

_____

_____

_____

_____

_____

_____

_____

_____

_____

_____

KINGDOM ACCOUNTABILITY QUESTION:

How is my life bringing honor to the Father's name?

_____

_____

_____

_____

_____

WEEK SEVEN, DAY TWO

YES,
I CAN WAIT

SCRIPTURE

I will praise You forever for what You have done. In the presence of Your faithful people, I will place my hope in Your name, for it is good.

Psalm 52:9

We are all influenced somewhat by the fast pace of life and the standards of the modern world. But our impatience to achieve, arrive, and accumulate can also lead to a lack of gratitude for what we have received from the Lord.

The Psalmist's thanksgiving is based on the assured, settled activity of God. This understanding of God's nature enables us to wait on the Father, always trusting in His timing and supply.

What does my impatience say to others about my Father?

_____

_____

_____

_____

_____

_____

_____

_____

_____

Today I had a chance to show what a contented life looks like:

_____

_____

_____

_____

_____

_____

_____

_____

_____

_____

_____

_____

_____

_____

KINGDOM ACCOUNTABILITY QUESTION:

How am I bringing reproach on my Father's name?

_____

_____

_____

_____

_____

WEEK SEVEN, DAY THREE

RIGHT WHERE THEY HURT

SCRIPTURE

"The LORD has anointed me to bring good news to the poor. He has sent me to bind up the brokenhearted, to proclaim liberty to the captives, and freedom to the prisoners."

Isaiah 61:1

The Lord Jesus quoted this section of Isaiah when He spoke in the synagogue in His hometown of Nazareth (Luke 4:18-19). His sole desire was to do the work of His Father's kingdom.

When we pray "Thy kingdom come," we are accepting His invitation to minister to the hurting in the power of the Spirit. The Father will show us kingdom moments all day long if we will simply make ourselves available to Him.

Who do I know that is afflicted, brokenhearted, enslaved?

_____

_____

_____

_____

_____

_____

_____

_____

_____

God opened my eyes to a kingdom opportunity today:

_____

_____

_____

_____

_____

_____

_____

_____

_____

_____

_____

_____

_____

_____

KINGDOM ACCOUNTABILITY QUESTION:

How well am I responding to kingdom opportunities?

_____

_____

_____

_____

WEEK SEVEN, DAY FOUR

STRAIGHT ANSWERS

SCRIPTURE

This is God's will, your sanctification: that you abstain from sexual immorality, so that each of you knows how to possess his own vessel in sanctification and honor.

1 Thessalonians 4:3-4

Sometimes we are guilty of talking about the Lord's will as if it is nebulous and somewhat hard to define. But the Bible is clear about God's desire for our moral purity. He wants us to be morally pure in both our mind and actions.

This is because the Father wants us to experience life abundantly. He has put boundaries in place to protect us from the evil that would rob us of abundance in every area of our lives.

As I think through the consequences of sexual sin. . .

_____

_____

_____

_____

_____

_____

_____

_____

_____

I've been seeing lately how hard self-control can be:

_____

_____

_____

_____

_____

_____

_____

_____

_____

_____

_____

_____

_____

KINGDOM ACCOUNTABILITY QUESTION:

How am I allowing God's will to be done in my life?

_____

_____

_____

_____

_____

WEEK SEVEN, DAY FIVE

COMPLETELY COVERED

SCRIPTURE

My God will supply all your needs according to His riches in glory in Christ Jesus. Now to our God and Father be glory forever and ever. Amen.

Philippians 4:19-20

"All your needs"—you can't get any more comprehensive than that! It may seem impossible that the Father is both willing and able to supply everything we need, but notice the resources He has available to Him! He supplies our needs "according to His riches in glory in Christ Jesus." That promise alone ought to bring our anxiety level down to zero. His power to provide is always greater than our need.

How small do my needs look when compared to God's power?

_____

_____

_____

_____

_____

_____

_____

_____

I didn't need all I wanted today. But all I needed, God gave:

_____

_____

_____

_____

_____

_____

_____

_____

_____

_____

_____

_____

_____

_____

_____

_____

KINGDOM ACCOUNTABILITY QUESTION:

How have I experienced God's provision in my life?

_____

_____

_____

_____

_____

WEEK SEVEN, DAY SIX

HE KNOWS,
HE UNDERSTANDS

SCRIPTURE

If we say, "We have no sin," we are deceiving ourselves, and the truth is not in us. If we confess our sins, He is faithful and righteous to forgive us our sins and to cleanse us from all unrighteousness.

1 John 1:8-9

The word *confess* comes from two Greek words meaning "to say the same thing." When we confess our sins, we are not revealing anything to our Father. We are agreeing with Him about our sin.

This truth should give us great freedom as we seek God's forgiveness for our sins. How comforting to know that His faithfulness and righteousness assure us that He will forgive and cleanse us.

God knows everything about me. How glad am I of that?

_____

_____

_____

_____

_____

_____

_____

_____

_____

I've never felt more secure in God's love than I do today:

_____

_____

_____

_____

_____

_____

_____

_____

_____

_____

_____

_____

_____

_____

KINGDOM ACCOUNTABILITY QUESTION:

For what do I need forgiveness? Who do I need to forgive?

_____

_____

_____

_____

FREE DELIVERY

SCRIPTURE

To Him who is able to protect you from stumbling and to make you stand in the presence of His glory, blameless and with great joy, to the only God our Savior, through Jesus Christ our Lord, be glory.

Jude 24-25

You're probably familiar with this profound benediction. But have you ever really taken its words seriously?

Stop and read it again. Praise the One who is able to keep us from stumbling, One fully equipped to "deliver us from evil." He will make us "stand in the presence of His glory, blameless with great joy," and we will worship Him forever in an eternal paradise where temptation can no longer touch us.

How can I thank You, Lord, for Your love and deliverance?

_____

_____

_____

_____

_____

_____

_____

_____

_____

Today I've given my life anew to God's delivering power:

_____
_____
_____
_____
_____
_____
_____
_____
_____
_____
_____
_____
_____
_____

KINGDOM ACCOUNTABILITY QUESTION:

How am I handling temptation? Am I experiencing victory?

_____
_____
_____
_____
_____

PRAYER

Congratulations!

You have made it through your *Prayer of Jesus Journal,* and I hope it's been for you a season of enrichment, encouragement, and enlightenment. No matter what you take away from this valuable experience, I know God will multiply the work He's begun or continued in you, that He will make sure every lesson you've learned finds a place of usefulness in your life.

You may already be wondering what you should do next. Let me offer a few very practical suggestions:

1) *Continue journaling.*

I pray that this process has been so rewarding, you will continue to adopt the discipline of prayer journaling. It doesn't require anything fancy. A simple notebook or calendar is more than sufficient for keeping track of what the Father is bringing to mind as you pray, as you read the Scriptures, as you interact with Him outside the boundaries of what you used to consider your "prayer time." Any time is now prayer time, right?

2) *Seek accountability.*

You may also want to consider finding a "kingdom accountability partner" to meet with on a regular basis to share what you are learning. You can use the seven questions from your prayer journal as a starting point for your accountability and prayer time. This kind of deliberate friendship will help keep you consistent and also allow you to share the insights God is giving you with someone else. You'll find that you will motivate one another to good works.

3) *Pray the prayer.*

I really want to encourage you to make the prayer of Jesus a lifestyle commitment. One of the main goals of this 7-week journaling experience was to help you establish a pattern that would become a sought-after habit. Begin each day with the prayer of Jesus on your lips and in your heart. Frequently reflect on the seven accountability questions that follow from the individual phrases of the prayer, even if you don't actually write out your thoughts.

4) *Start again.*

You may want to get another *Prayer of Jesus Journal* and start the process again immediately from the beginning. Consider at least doing this journaling process once a year to refresh your mind concerning your commitments and God's provision.

5) *Talk about it.*

Share with others what God is doing in your life. His purpose in communicating with you and providing for your needs is not merely to keep you contented and well-fed. He is showing and teaching you things that you need to express to others, especially those who don't realize that living a genuine, obedient Christian life is within their reach.

Thank you so much for taking your commitment to Jesus Christ seriously enough to spend this time in His model prayer. My prayer is that you will grow in your knowledge of Him and that you will experience His abundance every day.

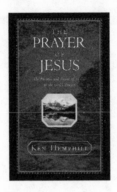

Clayton
Photography